Aural

Teshelle Combs

For Sarah, who blessed me with this idea and many others. Listen up.

Aural

Teshelle Combs

Wave

Undulation

With a point that is

Fixed.

It has the illusion of movement.

A thing imprisoned that

Frees us all.

Mellow

Smooth as it floats

And soft as it falls.

Velvet on the

Back of your hand.

A silhouette of water

On a summer afternoon.

Vibrations

When a child puts out their

Arms and turns and turns

Until they knock things off tables

And quite nearly fall on their faces,

But with particles instead of children

And hearts instead of tables.

Gurgle

A simmering.

A turning over.

Sound through liquid.

Hollow when in motion.

Frequency

That sound is

Material vibration

And constitutional

And repetitive

And not simply

A thing.

Infrasonic

Beneath us

In the dwelling

Of frequencies not

Our own

And not

For us.

Music

A sound, or many,

Put together or pulled apart

With the minimal intent of

Making something

That wasn't there before.

String

Shreds twisted

To make a thin length

And a thick sound

Much like the

Story of us.

Sonorous

Fullness added to depth

And not in a way that is

Invited

But imposed

And overwhelming.

Wind

The current.

Never to grasp

Or consume

But to witness it

Moving past your irrelevance.

Pitch

The precise rate

Of selected vibrations

Dictating the highs

And the lows

And the likes

And dislikes.

Lilting

A tuck and roll.

A rise and fall.

An over and under.

Sweet and exactly

What you want to hear.

Ultrasonic

The music made

Beyond us.

Whisper

Forsaking the tautening

Of the cords,

It is the intimacy

Of wind passing

Through patterns

Of bending lips.

Broken

No longer continuous,

No longer flowing,

And not always as bad

As they make it seem.

Grinding

Not the silence

That comes after it's

All through,

But the chilling haunt

That says it's near.

Tone

The way it is.

The color of the thing.

The texture of it.

The pull. The push.

The heart. The hold.

The way it feels.

The way it moves.

The way—regardless or regarded—it is.

Monotone

Unchanging, yet
Somehow still uncomforting.
It shows us the drudgery
Of exclusion.

Hushed

Not the silence itself

But the process of

It falling.

Muffled

Unsettling obstruction

And very rarely

On purpose.

To express that no one

Can understand

What we so desperately

Need to say.

Plaintive

When sorrow

Unfurls like

Petals in the morning

With no one to see.

Rhythm

Never has a system

Broken all the rules

The way you do.

Never has a pattern

Thrown us for a loop

And still proven true.

Staccato

A sudden separation.

Notes sliced apart

And placed side by side

Like stepping stones

In a rushing river.

Dulcet

Sweetness

In high doses and

Soothing to the

Senses.

Rich

Luxurious in tone

And weighted

With revelation.

Full and forceful

And sure of its value.

Brassy

Blaring and stomping

Through the streets like

The pavement is a party.

There is no choice

But to listen.

Like it or not.

Raucous

It is in itself

A disturbance.

Where there was first

Nothing,

There is a wild and rattled

Unnerving.

Shrill

Pitched too high

For reaching

And too loud

For pleasure.

Too much.

Always just a little too much.

Caterwaul

From a dark place,

A rising, shrieking

Howl

That slithers up the spine

And brings the cold.

Creak

When there is motion

Or something is stepped on

Or pulled at,

And it resists,

As we all do.

Drone

One—

And only one—

That goes

And does not stop.

It is the fly in your ear.

It is the buzz overhead.

It ties together

And sets apart.

Screech

No roundness

And no curvature.

No ambling

And no gentility.

More of a pierce

Through quiet hills.

Rumble

Resonance

Beneath us that

Doesn't end.

A curious

Flow.

A sound that shakes

The earth.

Euphonic

Words like art.

Words like music.

Phonetic for pleasure.

Ripples in the water

Arranged in perfect order.

Thrum

The sound of life

And the rhythm it makes

Pulsing through us.

Wheeze

Air forcing past

An obstruction

And whistling as it goes,

Just as we do

When we get through

But just barely.

Pop

An explosion

But just a little one.

Not always deliberate

And usually a surprise.

Balance

Tones spread

Like arms wide open

And neither shifting

Away from where

They were meant to be.

Rasp

The grating of a sound

As it passes through

To wherever it's going.

Tempo

The again and so on

Of the rhythm.

More or less

Or in between.

A continually welcomed lurch.

Bright

Light always is

Elevating above the rest.

It reaches us,

Or rather we reach up

To hear it.

Articulate

Not sound unwitting.

No longer simple

And not slapped together,

But intelligent and

In conversation.

Howling

If a craving

Were a sound.

If a need were in waves.

If misery and desire

Could be hurled at the moon.

Pierce

It goes into, yes,

But it also goes through.

At times, it administers

Or leaves a deposit

Of some auxiliary thing.

But it first and finally leaves

A hole.

Decay

After every attack,

When it is all over

And the sound has done its job

And run its course,

There is inevitable

Decay.

Crisp

Light.

Like snow on green grass,

Like the first bite of an apple,

Droplets still on its skin.

The sizzle of a cymbal

When you hit it just right.

Dry

It is what it is.

There is no swollen echo,

No twisting reverberation.

No crunch of distortion.

No fat flop. No damp dark.

It is simply itself.

Dull

Sludge

That slops

Always downhill,

Covered in leaves

And clumped in mud.

Fat

Taking from one

And feeding the other

Until it is full.

Taking from the other

And feeding the one

Until it, too, is full.

Grainy

Raw and grating.

We feel the coarseness

Against our senses.

We taste the gravel

On our tongues.

Lush

Not passive.

A presence of authority

And freedom.

Rolling plains and

Wheat as far as the eye can see.

It owns itself.

57

Muddy

Not only messy,

But weak.

Not only slipping

But smeared.

A wash of

What should not be.

Range

The stretch

From the top of it all

To the bottom of it all.

Like a mountain

Being scaled.

Buzz

A murmur.

A cacophony of flapping.

A zipping through the air.

Sometimes welcome and

Sometimes a nuisance.

Saturation

A flood of warmth

And no more room

To absorb it.

You float in the

Fullness of it,

And it in you.

Tonal

The sound

Of a sound

And the nature

Of its nature.

Weight

In the very deepest place

And still in control.

For there is power in substance,

Even when it lies low.

Ambience

Not the thing itself

Nor the essence of it

But the impression

It makes in the space

The sound takes.

Transient

To realize

When it hits

That you are

On the edge of a sound

And very alive.

Sweet

Imprint.

Inculcation.

The rise of a gentle sweep

Like wind across open land.

The harmony of each orb

In its destined spiral.

The taste of a sound

When it is seared into memory.

The fulfillment of it

Crawling over your skin.

The reorientation of your heartbeat.

The appropriation of the thing we call

Soul.

The measure of feeling immortal

And knowing we are not.

Followed, finally and perpetually,

By foundational gratitude.

More Works by Teshelle Combs

Let There Be Nine Series

- *Let There Be Nine Vol 1*: **Enneagram Poetry**
- *Let There Be Nine Vol 2*: **Enneagram Poetry**

For Series: Words laced together on behalf of an idea, a place, a world.

- **For Her**
- **For Him**
- **For Them**
- **For Us**

Love Bad Series: Poems About Love. Not Love Poems.

- **Love Bad**
- **Love Bad More**
- **Love Bad Best**

Core Series

Ava is the kind of girl who knows what's real and what isn't. Nothing in life is fair. Nothing is given freely. Nothing is painless. Every foster kid can attest to those truths, and Ava lives them every day. But when she meets a family of dragon shifters and is chosen to join them as a rider, her very notion of reality is shaken. She doesn't believe she can let her guard down. She doesn't think she can let them in—especially not the reckless, kind-eyed Cale. To say yes to him means he would be hers—her dragon and her companion—for life. But what if Ava has no life left to give?

The System Series

1 + 1 = Dead. That's the only math that adds up when you're in the System. Everywhere Nick turns, he's surrounded by the inevitability of his own demise at the hands of the people who stole his life from him. That is, until those hands deliver the bleeding, feisty, eye-rolling Nessa Parker. Tasked with keeping his new partner alive, Nick must face all the ways he's died and all the things he's forgotten.

Nessa might as well give up. The moment she gets into that car, the moment she lays her hazel eyes on her new partner, her end begins. It doesn't matter that Nick Masters can slip through time by computing mathematical algorithms in his mind. It doesn't matter how dark and handsome and ir-resistibly cold he is. Nessa has to defeat her own shadows. Together and alone, Nick and Nessa make sense of their senseless fates and fight for the courage to change it all. Even if it means the System wins and they end up...well...dead.

Standalone Short Books:

The Keymaker

TheRealOnes

CREATE THROUGH THE FEAR

The Midnight Journal

Contact Teshelle Combs

Instagram @TeshelleCombs

Email: teshellecombs@gmail.com